BUSINESS BESTIES

How to Win BIG in Business with Your Best Friends!

By

KODDI DUNN

Business and Personal Development Strategist

Copyright © 2024 Koddi Dunn.

All Rights Reserved

Table of Contents

Preface 1
The Big Idea 4
   TIP 1: Energy-Synergy 7
   TIP 2: Managing Expectations 13
   TIP 3: Division Of Labor (Part I) 27
   Division of Labor (Part II): Time 30
   TIP: 5: Daily Commitments 37
   TIP: 6: Development Budget 41
   TIP: 7: The Wild-Wild Web… 44
   TIP 8: Everything shouldn't be free… 47
Recap I 49
   TIP: 9: Letting your baby grow. 51
   TIP: 10: Who's Selling to Whom 53
   TIP: 11: Advertising & Promotions 55
   TIP: 12 – Social Media Marketing 57
   TIP: 13: Internet Marketing 61
   TIP: 14 – Famous Friends 63
Recap II 64
   TIP: 15: All About the Benjamins 65
   TIP: 16: Ugh. The Legal Stuff. 68

TIP: 17: Who's Got Bank 70

TIP: 18: I'm Watching You 74

TIP: 19: The Money Tree 77

TIP: 20: Call My Lawyer! 80

TIP: 21: Customer Disputes 82

TIP: 22: Client Accessibility 85

TIP: 23: The Truth About Taxes 89

TIP: 24: The Right Way to Quit 92

TIP: 25: Code of Conduct 95

7 Core Business Values 98

   Core Business Value I - Intergrity 99

   Core Business Value II: Self-Discipline 102

   Core Business Value III: Freedom of Thought 107

   Core Business Value IV: Consideration 109

   Core Business Value V: Community Success 111

   Core Business Value VI: Transparency & Authenticity .. 112

   Core Business Values VII: Respect 113

The Final Warning: 116

   About the Author: 125

Preface

Hello there! I'm Koddi Dunn, serial entrepreneur and top business executive. I've written this book to help you WIN big in business with your best friends! This book is all about making your business partnerships profitable and sensible. It's a friend's guide to business consulting and collaboration, and it's the real deal.

As far back as I can remember, I've been the super productive friend in my group with a strong independent entrepreneurial streak. You know, the one always rushing to a business meeting and missing brunch. Whether I'm launching a new product, improving an existing one, or finding a new angle on a classic to make a profit, I've always had an unstoppable business drive. It's been stronger than any social activity. In fact, the only way my spouse got my attention over a decade ago was by asking about a business product on my social media page. I'm just that business savvy.

Over the years, as I've expanded my relationships and friendships, I've met many friends who also have that extra business drive like me. They respect my business skills and understand my expertise. Because of this synergy, they want to connect with me or grow their ideas with my help.

Twenty-plus years of collaborating and consulting with my best friends have taught me some tough and even heart-breaking lessons. So, believe me, I have a few insights about partnerships that you might not have considered but should, before moving forward with your next big deal.

This is a great book for anyone looking to take their business to the next level through partnerships, especially with someone they know well or love.

I used to give this advice out like candy. Anyone could call me and say, "Hey Koddi, I have an idea or a concept, and I'm working with someone on it… what are your thoughts?" I would always help, and after spending countless hours on consulting calls year after year, I realized there was a specific set of questions and concerns that came up every single time.

In the excitement of a new idea, certain details are often glossed over, and crucial matters ignored. My business experience has taught me that you can miss important things in the thrill of a new venture. If you don't address these essentials upfront, they can destroy your business and possibly your relationship later on, and that's not what you want.

If this new venture is a good idea and a great concept, you want it to work, and I want you to win.

That's one of the main reasons Business Besties is such a great book for anyone starting a new business deal or opportunity. Let me guide you through the tricky issues and talking points that might seem uncomfortable at first. Feel free to blame me when a topic is too tough or touchy to tackle. Use my experiences as your resource, so you can achieve great results and perhaps even build a stronger business connection with your partner(s) later.

One more thing—I believe conversations should be a two-way street, so I invite you to share your thoughts with me online. Like my Facebook page or follow me on any of the social media platforms listed in the back of this book. If you want direct consultation services, email me at koddi@pinkrosemarketing.com, and I will make sure we get connected.

You've got this, and I've got you. *Friend, Let's get started!*

The Big Idea

It was a usual relaxed Sunday afternoon. I was at home with my two youngest kids, lounging and watching TV when my phone rang. It was my older sister, sounding excited and talking quickly, signaling something exciting. Making sure my little ones were engrossed in their movie, I quietly walked down the hall to my office.

"Koddi!" she said urgently. "I hope I'm not interrupting, but I need some *business* advice..." Hearing the slight disappointment in my voice as I responded with, "What's going on?" made her tone less enthusiastic. Weekends usually meant uninterrupted time with my family, but my work often involved constant consulting on others' projects. Today, I just wanted to relax with my loved ones.

Being aware of my fatigue, she said, "No worries. I'll call you tomorrow." Click. The call ended abruptly, and I returned to my kids down the hall. I only made it as far as the kitchen when the phone rang again. As expected, it was my sister, calling back within minutes, once again unable to contain her excitement. This time, she was determined. I chuckled and turned back to my home office. My relaxing "no work" Sunday was now officially interrupted by the opportunity to offer business advice to someone thrilled about a potential new partnership. It was fine I knew she needed my help, and I was happy to provide it.

When dealing with entrepreneurs, especially newcomers, it's important to be cautious and gentle when discussing their ideas. They may have faced skeptics before reaching out to you, and they likely have their own internal concerns, even if they're not voicing them loudly. Those concerns are what drive their excitement.

Beyond the excitement of a new opportunity or dream to earn money, entrepreneurs often hear doubts creeping in quietly. Their sudden burst of activity is their way of pushing those doubts aside. Protecting their new business idea is crucial, so adding negativity to the conversation won't help. It could even offend or hurt them. Instead, it's important to address their concerns while also considering the practical aspects, balancing potential gains with possible risks. But I was familiar with all of this. I had given this kind of advice countless times before. I knew that as a mentor, sister, and business strategist, I needed to step into all these roles at once. I grabbed my freshly brewed cup of mandarin hot tea, a newfound favorite, and settled down at my desk to share in my sister's excitement.

As she started describing the opportunity, I reminded myself to proceed cautiously. She was incredibly excited about this new idea. I began to think that perhaps this phone call and chance to offer advice could be the key to her next big success. I listened closely as she explained the concept, her role, and her potential partner's plan. When it was my turn to respond, I spoke from the heart. Words of care, concern, and connection flowed naturally. By the end of our conversation, I felt drained but satisfied. She was energized, and my kids' movie had just finished. But the story doesn't end there. I knew there were more people like her out there— folks who just needed someone to listen to and a trustworthy person to believe *in* their ideas. More people who could benefit from what I've learned, whether they know me personally or not. So, just like my older sister calling me on a weekend and pulling me away from my kids, let's dive in and discuss how to make your business thrive. Welcome to The Business Besties.

Hey best friend, *Are you ready?* **Cool.**

TIP 1: Energy-Synergy

You're at the local PTA meeting, chatting with a mix of new faces and familiar annual attendees. During a conversation about your recent activities and future plans, you discover a shared enthusiasm with Carrie, another parent in the group. Both of you share fantastic ideas, high energy, and a mutual desire for some accountability. Despite having separate families, individual challenges, and personal aspirations, today marks the beginning of a newfound connection between the two of you.

The question I get asked the most is, "How can you turn unique ideas into successful collaborations?" I understand. You want to do it, but you don't have the time, resources, or availability to do everything yourself?

Oh, wouldn't it be great to clone yourself and have a billionaire like Uncle Bill Gates on speed dial? He could fund your dreams, and you and your clone could blitz through all those overwhelming tasks in record time! In just a few years, maybe even months, you'd be swimming in money, enough to buy beach houses and lakefront properties. Your idea is that good. But turning it into reality is tough. You're stuck between believing you can do it and feeling overwhelmed. This is where many entrepreneurial teams lose their direction. But don't worry. As a seasoned business owner with two decades of experience in major markets, I've been right where you are. Guiding you from idea to execution is my specialty.

Now, the big question is, "How do we get started, Koddi? I'm ready to make serious money!" The answer to that question is a bit complicated, but don't worry, we'll cover it and more in the upcoming chapters.

However, the first step when considering a major collaboration is to gauge the energy. I often discuss this with my consulting clients as "Energy-Synergy". It's a crucial assessment because if you're not enthusiastic or don't share a common dream, this "BIG" business idea will fizzle out. I believe dreams drive us, and if your dream doesn't resonate with the other person, you're already at a disadvantage. In short, if my dream doesn't inspire you naturally, this partnership won't succeed.

I grew up going to church weekly, and often use faith-based analogies. One story that might illustrate the energy-synergy concept is from Luke 1:41, about Mary and Elizabeth. The Bible describes how when Mary, who was pregnant, visited Elizabeth, who was also pregnant and six months along, Elizabeth's baby "leaped in her womb" at Mary's greeting. This shows how what was inside both of them connected on a deep level.

They connected and supported each other, inspiring one another along their respective paths. Energy-synergy is especially crucial when starting a new project. Before anything else, it's essential to do an energy-synergy check. This means ensuring that both parties aren't just excited by the conversation, but genuinely passionate about the project.

I often tell my clients that my purpose is what motivates me every morning and keeps me going after a long, challenging day. If our project isn't aligned with my purpose, it won't be my top priority when I'm tired or frustrated.

When life gets busy and there aren't enough hours in the day, I may not have the internal motivation to prioritize *your* needs. If it doesn't align with my greater purpose, I may not feel compelled to act. While it might have started out enjoyable and exciting to work with you, when I'm tired or distracted, only tasks that align with my purpose can grab my attention and keep me focused. This means "our project" might end up taking a back seat.

Life is precious, and time is valuable. It's important to align our energy and purpose so we don't waste the most valuable investment anyone can make - *time*.

Moreover, if we're not heading in the same direction, this new business venture, no matter how brilliant the idea, won't succeed. If my "dream train" is heading north towards Michigan hypothetically, and your "dream train" is heading south towards Florida, we'll never intersect. We're simply moving in different directions, which doesn't mean one of us is wrong. It just means we're not aligned. Before investing time, money, and effort, it's crucial to connect with someone whose purpose and direction match yours.

Don't spend your time and effort on someone who isn't fully supportive of your dreams or doesn't believe in them as much as you do. If you don't feel a connection or synergy, then maybe it was just a pleasant chat, but not the right **partnership**. Keep this idea in the concept phase and move on, friend.

You have to advocate for yourself and not be afraid to speak up and say, "Hey, you know what? I love this concept and it's a great idea, but right now, I'm not sure I'm ready to move forward."

I think any mature business partner would respect someone who speaks up and tells the truth early on. There's nothing worse than regretting pushing forward with a business plan when deep down, you knew you weren't ready - but didn't speak up for yourself. **That**

hesitation can create resistance and obstacles that sabotage the idea later on. It's important to be honest from the start and avoid self-sabotage, later.

You need to stand up for yourself and not be afraid to say, "Hey, you know what? I really like this idea, but right now, I'm not sure I'm ready to move forward."

I believe any mature business partner would respect someone who speaks up and tells the truth early on. There's nothing worse than regretting going ahead with a business plan when deep down, you knew you weren't ready but didn't speak up for yourself. *That* hesitation can create resistance and obstacles that hold you back. You might end up sabotaging the business idea only because you didn't speak up and be honest from the start.

Sometimes, fear can be overcome with logic, action, and faith. But other times, it's your gut feeling or intuition sending you a warning that this might not be the right path for you.

Whatever your inner voice tells you, listen carefully. Trust its wisdom, and the right opportunities and next steps will unfold naturally. Whether you find peace pursuing a new business passion or decide to wait because the timing isn't right, follow what feels right <u>for you.</u>

Once you've checked your **energy alignment** and completed a self-assessment, you and your business partner are ready to move forward. You've found that your energies match, your dreams align, and your purposes are on the same track. You both believe this business idea is promising and worth pursuing!

Great! Keep reading to discover your next steps.

However, if you're facing a difficult conversation, reach out to my team for consulting advice. If you're unsure how to end a partnership gracefully, we can help. How you finish things can be as important as how they start. It's wise not to burn bridges you may need later.

Also, check out our Bonus Companion Book: "30 Tough Conversation Starters" available on our website. It can guide you in speaking your mind with tact and preserving relationships. Get your copy now – you'll be glad you did!

TIP 2: Managing Expectations

Next, I'm going to share the stages to consider for moving forward and achieving business success. One key factor is setting the **right business expectations.**

Friend, what do you want from this? What's your end game? What's your dream result? Are you aiming to make a lot of money to buy a beach house? Do you want to tour the world as a phenomenal, sought-after speaker or future business maverick? Or are you looking to launch a product that can be replicated, leading to business trainings and ideas beyond your usual boundaries? Honestly, what is your end game? What are your business expectations? What do you both want from this venture? Think it over carefully and write it down. Then, connect and discuss your dreams with your potential partner. Let's call her Carrie; you know, the lady from the PTA meeting at your kid's school? Connect with Carrie and say, "Okay, here's what I want from this..." Then, let her share her goals as well. Be prepared for whatever she says and give her dreams the same respect as your own.

Friend, sometimes people don't want all the money in the world. Maybe they're just looking for a comfortable lifestyle and financial stability. If your dream and effort level is aiming for seven figures, but *they* don't share the same work ethic, drive, or ambition, you might hit a snag. So, it's important to set the right expectations upfront.

What results are we aiming for? What does having a lot of money mean to you? Is it $100,000? $500,000? Or a million dollars? Depending on your debt load and goals, these answers may differ greatly. Based on that, you and Carrie can hopefully reach an agreement or at least a mutual understanding of what truly constitutes business success.

If a million dollars per person per year is the goal, discuss what that looks like. Ensure your business model includes a profitable method to potentially generate that kind of ROI (return on investment) over the next three to five years. It's important to sit down together and do the math.

Another example is this: What if you and Carrie aim to make a total of half a million dollars over the next five years? That's $100,000 a year, or $50,000 per person. This means your business model should generate and pay out $50,000 to each of you after expenses. So, if you've agreed on that amount, let's figure out how to achieve it.

This is the meeting where you officially set the proper expectation for your desired results.

The conversation may start as a frank and honest discussion about money, but you and Carrie quickly realize that aligning on money might be the easy part. Defining roles and responsibilities is where things can get tricky. So, pack your patience and get ready for the rollercoaster ride of what comes next.

Finding the Win-Win

After setting your financial goals, the next step in managing expectartions is to find a "win-win" situation. Everyone brings different assets and knowledge to the table, so you need to ensure that success for them is also success for you. Define what a "win" means. It may seem silly or obvious, but it is extremely important.

A close friend of mine, Ariel, wanted to add coaching to her business development company. She was a pro at websites and graphics and wanted to teach others how to achieve her results. However, whenever she tried to launch a website development course, people would stall due to a lack of focus or self-esteem issues. Being resourceful, Ariel decided to team up with a life coach. She could offer clients practical knowledge about running a graphics-based business, while the life coach could help keep them motivated. Ariel thought this partnership would create a successful business model. When she discussed it with me, it sounded great! Finding a life coach looking for new clients, whose coaching packages you can add to your service, gives you an advantage in the marketplace.

I told her, "Ariel, go for it! You're getting more clients by adding something unique that ensures your clients do the work and get the results they want. If your clients are getting results, they're happy. For the life coach, partnering with you brings more business and exposure, boosting thier bottom line. Ariel, this is a win-win!" I encouraged her to have the tough "what if this all goes wrong" conversations early on, but driven by ambition, Ariel didn't take that part of my advice.

The energy and synergy initially worked well as both people started to develop their innovative "business coaching product". This is the kind of partnership you want, where roles are clearly defined and understood. Everyone knows what needs to be done and who is responsible. It's a textbook example of a win-win situation. However, as Ariel would learn, their partnership eventually hit a few snags. They failed to review some classic principles for a solid partnership, and Ariel eventually decided to end their business arrangement. She later told me she felt a bit used.

"Koddi, I feel like I'm doing all the work. I built the website, pay for the advertising, and develop the social media campaigns. But my partner just shows up for the training sessions, gives a few pep talks and hands out brochures about her coaching services, then leaves, sometimes before the session is even over!" Ariel complained during our consulting meeting.

I tried to hide my "I told you so..." look for as long as I could, but it was true. I had advised her to slow down and handle the logistics before investing so much time and energy into this partnership. Potential is great, but we need to be honest about the risks. When we get blinded by potential profits, we can get taken advantage of by anyone. Friend beware! You're not getting a win-win if you feel like you're doing all the work! Eventually, the excitement fades, real life sets in, and you WILL get tired. When fatigue sets in, frustration follows, and then we're not being our true selves.

Ariel's life coach partner wasn't a bad person, but they didn't set clear expectations. Ariel didn't really consider the time, focus, and resources she needed for the business to work. If they had discussed their roles in detail and maybe even assigned a value to them, Ariel could have requested a larger share of the profits. I think that if Ariel had been earning a commission for any new clients the life coach got because of her efforts, their partnership might have lasted.

However, Ariel no longer felt like she was winning and started to resent her partner, feeling taken advantage of by them. Was she? Maybe. I think it's debatable.

Acceptable work behavior and commitment levels must be discussed and balanced in order to ensure longevity in business.

By the end, Ariel missed the mark and lost a potentially good business opportunity because it no longer felt balanced to her. However, that's not entirely her partner's fault. Ariel jumped in without considering the costs, and it turned out to be a big mistake.

Friend, make sure you define the "win-win" for both you and your partner upfront. Clearly discuss the rules, roles, and responsibilities. What will your role be in this partnership? What are you expected to do, and what do you expect from your partner? If you're using your talents to launch and grow the business, are you emotionally mature enough to speak up when you feel unbalanced or to pull back when other aspects of your life are affected?

I think Ariel could have saved her partnership if she had communicated her concerns about her partner's work ethic and maybe hired an outside vendor for the most time-consuming tasks. It was silly of her to let herself get continually bothered when the workload felt unbalanced.

Ariel didn't understand the importance of setting proper expectations to avoid conflicts and bad results. Also, not being able to share her thoughts when frustrated might have hurt her reputation. An honest conversation with her partner could have changed the outcome, but without talking it out, they both walked away disappointed.

Another story I will share is this one. I received an email from Samantha, a young fitness instructor, sharing her business journey. Samantha wanted to expand her fitness business online but lacked technical skills. She noticed other trainers gaining large social media followings but didn't know how to do it herself.

Luckily, Samantha found a trusted friend to partner with. Together, they created an online business plan. Samantha took on much of the initial work: recording videos, designing training programs, and hiring talent for the videos. As she worked on the project, Samantha grew passionate about making a positive impact on people's lives. Her goal was to help others achieve fitness and maintain their health through education and lifestyle changes.

Once all the recording and preparation were done, Samantha handed the recorded segments to her business partner. It was their job to organize them into an online course. Samantha hoped this would allow people to sign up, complete the program, and leave with a plan for long-term results. Their partnership is a great example of knowing their roles and responsibilities. After a few consulting sessions with me on generating monthly recurring revenue, Samantha and her partner were on track to achieve lasting success.

That's how clear role definition should work. It's not about saying, "I'll handle web development and you manage social media, but I'll take Instagram because I'm more familiar with it." That casual approach to who does what can lead to confusion. It's crucial to establish clear roles and responsibilities based on agreed assignments and desired outcomes.

For instance, if your role involves managing our business's social media accounts, document your expectations clearly. Define what "managing social media" means to each of you to ensure mutual understanding going forward. Don't make assumptions!

Let's go deeper here. If you're responsible for our business's social media, I expect you to post engaging content, respond to interactions, and actively work to increase our following. If this feels overwhelming, let's find a way to make our social media strategy work better and meet our expectations.

On the other hand, if you're assigned to manage our social media because of your role in web development, but you feel too busy to do it, and you keep seeing me posting on my personal social media because I enjoy it... you might get frustrated with my online activity. You might think, "If she has time to post on her personal page, why isn't she posting on our business page?" I could argue that it's not my job or responsibility, *it's yours*.

We might find it necessary to revisit our roles and responsibilities and consider transferring "our" social media management to me. But you need to be open and confident in communicating that unmet expectation to me. Be transparent and say, "Friend, this web development is taking up a lot of my time and responsibility. I could use some extra help." Then I might respond, "No worries! I can handle it. Outsourcing our social media posting costs about $100 a month. Let me locate a vendor." Alternatively, I could say, "Sure, I can take care of it. Just send me the information. I've got it covered!"

Since we had a conversation to update our roles and responsibilities, we can now focus on the next big thing.

Side Bar: Personal Accountability Metrics (PAM)

Understanding and discussing what I call PAM, or **Personal Accountability Metrics**, helps keep your business running smoothly. There needs to be proof of work, *a trust but verify system*. It's not personal, and you won't take it as an attack if you're doing your job. If you get offended when I ask basic questions, it raises red flags! Your overreaction signals that something is wrong, and that means, friend, we're about to have **PAM** problems.

As a mom, I've noticed that emotional breakdowns are often clever tactics of manipulation and distraction. My youngest son, Jaden, who is in elementary school at that time of this writing, illustrated this perfectly one day.

While I was working in my home office, Jaden came running downstairs in a full emotional breakdown - screaming, crying, and terribly upset! Normally, Jaden is a reasonable and calm child, so I knew something strange was happening. Through his tears, he told me why he was upset… *with his father.*

Moments into his story, I realized Jaden's account was one-sided. He only told me about his punishment, leaving out what he had done wrong. It turned out *he* was at fault and was going to lose access to his technology as a consequence.

He didn't want to talk about what he had done, just about getting scolded by his dad. I knew that tactic and said, "Son, you're child number six out of the seven we've raised. I'm not responding to your reaction. When you calm down and want to talk about what you did wrong, I'm ready. Until then, this situation and outcome is a direct result of your choices."

My response stopped him completely. He thought I would be an easier advocate, and my lack of perceived desire to arbitrate made him even more upset. I waited a few more moments as he sat there crying, peeking through his tears to see if I was looking. Then I said to him, "What did you do that caused this?" Finally, he told me. As he spoke, he became calmer. Although he wasn't happy, he had to admit that his dad and I had been right. He had broken a rule and faced the expected (and predetermined) consequence.

You know, I'm finding that with adults, it's often the same. When people call and they're screaming and yelling, and making a scene, many times they're not trying to talk over you... they're trying to talk over themselves. There's something in the back of their mind saying, "You know what you did was wrong," or "You know you didn't do what you were supposed to do. **They aren't trying to be louder than you – they are trying to be louder than PAM.**

In business, we need to recognize that discussing accountability can be tough because nobody likes being held responsible, especially if things aren't going well. Going back to the original example, if it's now my responsibility to manage our social media and I'm not doing it, meaning I'm not posting and we're not seeing any growth or results, it's fair for you, as my business partner, to bring it up. But because people naturally resist criticism, expect me to react defensively, shifting the focus away from myself, just like little Jaden did.

At that point, it's important to be discerning enough to recognize when someone is trying to sidestep discussing their own efforts or lack of results by taking you on an emotional rollercoaster.

Listen, I didn't mention sales; I talked about results. If I'm not delivering results, you have every right, and honestly, it's your responsibility, to ask me what's going on. But be ready, because naturally, I might not want to admit it! I'll probably come up with excuses or even get defensive. However, in business, accountability is crucial. You might need to say, "Hey, I thought our Instagram should be gaining 100 followers a week, but it's not. What do you think is the issue?" Approach it with a problem-solving mindset, not an accusatory one. Resist being negative, and always aim for a positive outcome.

For instance, you might also approach the conversation with a non-judgmental tone and ask, "Hey, it looks like our Instagram growth has slowed down. How can I assist?" Be open to reviewing and adjusting your goals as necessary. Have we set an unrealistic target? Are we being too ambitious? Perhaps aiming for 100 new social media followers per week is too high. It might be more realistic to aim for 10 or 20 new followers weekly and post every other day instead.

Opting to discuss your concerns with empathy and genuine care can help you find a solution **without sparking a heated argument and potentially losing a friend.**

If I were having this conversation, I would ensure my partner knows about new technology and resources that can help us improve our results. For example, concerning social media, I'd make sure they're using the latest tools for using " trending hashtags" to connect our account with potential new customers. The key is to come to the conversation with solutions. Offer possible answers, and not just a list of problems.

The Bible says in Matthew 11:6 (KJV), "Blessed is he who is not offended in me". When establishing accountability, avoid a tone that triggers defensiveness. Instead, seek to understand any obstacles they may face so you can achieve a positive outcome *together.*

Friend, for our business to succeed, accountability in our roles and responsibilities is crucial.

TIP 3: Division Of Labor (Part I)

Next, let's discuss how tasks are divided in your new partnership. Depending on your type of business, this can vary greatly.

Some of you may have already done the groundwork and are now seeking exposure. A potential partner might say, "I have the platform, but I need this extra component to make it work!" Therefore, the division of labor might not be equal initially. However, it's crucial for both partners to contribute regularly. In my business with my husband, I handle about ninety percent of our marketing. I create and execute campaigns, decide on content, and plan where to promote them.

He represents us in some campaigns and oversees our technical support team. We both focus heavily on product launches, training, and sales. Depending on the type of training needed, clients might book sessions with either of us. Technical matters usually go to his team, while marketing and sales go to mine. To ensure our business runs smoothly, we stick to clear roles and avoid overlapping responsibilities.

If we receive a training request that involves sales information, it comes to me and my team because that's our expertise. Requests for technical information go to my husband's team, even if I know the answer. I prefer to let his team handle it because it's not my role.

Handling technical support issues isn't part of my responsibilities. I focus on my own tasks to avoid burnout and stay effective in my role.

With over twenty years as an entrepreneur, I've learned that if I spend all my energy on technical support, I won't be mentally ready to handle sales questions or issues when they arise.

I've also learned that division of labor doesn't equate to knowledge alone. Even if you know something, it's important to respect each person's role and not overstep boundaries. This respect ensures peace and accountability. You never want a client to say, "Carrie told me X, Y, Z..." if it wasn't my responsibility, as this can contradict Carrie and undermine her authority. Such interference, especially with clients, can frustrate my partner and create resentment. While I didn't mean to cause offense, my actions beyond my role can complicate their work and make customers doubt my partner's ability to deliver.

If my partner can't handle or isn't qualified to resolve a client's issue, it's crucial that I consult with them before stepping in. By following the proper channels, we greatly reduce the chance of misunderstandings. It also prevents customers from pitting one partner against the other to get what they want, a common tactic. Knowing what's been discussed, offered, and agreed upon beforehand ensures smooth customer interactions and increases the likelihood of repeat business or client referrals for your company.

Division of Labor (Part II): Time

One of the first aspects to clarify in division of labor is time. It's crucial to be very clear about how much time each of us needs to dedicate to the project. If we've agreed on one hour per day, that totals five hours from Monday to Friday. It might also be helpful to schedule a recap session on Friday afternoons to review our progress, any challenges we've encountered, and to plan for the following week based on our goals and objectives.

Time management is crucial. If it's not balanced, **fatigue** leads to frustration, affecting how you respond, something you want to avoid. Ensure time is properly divided to prevent this.

Division of Labor: Duration of Development (Part III)

Another key aspect of division of labor is the development timeline. Some people have excellent ideas but never launch them because they spend too much time brainstorming or getting stuck in the planning phase.

Development involves bringing the concept together, but staying in this phase indefinitely yields no real results. Therefore, part of our division of labor should include discussing how long we'll spend planning versus when we'll actually start implementing our ideas.

Honestly, I'm comfortable giving six weeks for the production and creative development of any business concept. I've been a key player in several very successful business launches over the past few years, and I believe typically that six weeks is the maximum time we should spend on product development because extending beyond that often leads to idleness and slower productivity.

Consequently, speeding up the process and launching before six weeks makes you prone to mistakes that could be avoided with more time. However, six weeks from our initial conversation, we should be starting. We should be up and running, not in six months, but in six weeks. We need to be on the same page because, based on your life responsibilities, if that doesn't work for you, we need to discuss and make adjustments that suit both of us.

Also, don't get lost in endless development and "perfectionist" excuses, because that's an easy trap to fall into and it happens more often than you think. Many great ideas and business plans end up in the "someday" pile because they lacked follow-through or had flexible timelines with no real deadlines. Friend, take your future seriously and prioritize your time so you can deliver when it's time to produce results.

Often, when brainstorming over the phone with a new partner, we talk about a great idea, and then one of us gets another call. "Hey, I'm going to call you back!" is the familiar phrase that signals the end of what could have been something great. *Why?* Because I never called you back to discuss the idea. Now it's the next week, complete with a new set of life challenges I must solve. Before you know it, another week has gone by, and we've done nothing with our idea. Nothing! A great concept dies off because we were stagnant and distracted.

We failed to prioritize our lives and set aside the time needed to develop our concept and advance our business idea. Even if it's a virtual call, phone call, or coffee shop visit, reserve the time needed to collaborate. This way, you're creating metrics for your development and maintaining that activity pattern. You must do this each week as you committed and review your progress accordingly. Once you complete what you planned, your momentum will shift toward productivity, and that alone can work miracles in helping you stay focused and get your product to the finish line.

The duration of development is important. It's a small factor, but failing to stick to a timeline will leave you on the couch in shock while someone else pitches your idea to TV investors or serves customers that should have been yours at their new local shop.

TIP: 4: LIFE HAPPENS.

The next factor in Business Besties is a reminder that **life happens**. It's about more than just events occurring; it's about having a plan for when they do. If your partner gets sick, if you get sick, if you need to go out of town, or if something else important requires your attention, it must be addressed quickly, honestly, and effectively.

Right now, I'm in the thick of putting three kids through college, guiding another into adulthood, homeschooling one, and helping another through high school, all while raising a toddler. Friend, I'm **swamped**. Recognizing my current life demands means it wouldn't be wise for me to take on a new business partnership right now. Ideas are coming my way, but declining all business invitations is the right decision because my focus needs to be on my "Mommy" duties.

I can't focus on any new venture right now because my priority is getting all my kids through school and on to success. However, in the fall or maybe next summer, as our family adjusts to a new normal, I might be open to exploring additional revenue streams. My response isn't a "no," it's just a "not right now." Although they may seem the same, they are two completely different answers.

Understanding this reality helps us protect both our friendship and our expectations. If I don't explain what's happening in my life to my business partner, I'm not being fair to them. **Effective communication means I need to quickly and accurately explain my availability before we go into business.**

If my availability changes after we start our company, I must be as honest and quick as possible about my new time constraints.

As my business partner, I hope you understand, but that's *your* decision to make. **Denying you the right to choose is where many partnerships fail.** I hope you understand that a major life event has happened for me. While I am distracted right now, it won't always be this way. This is just how things are for now, so if you want to enter or remain in partnership with me, you need to be aware of my current limitations. Saying, "Okay Koddi, I'm going to wait 30 days," or "I'll wait 60 days and then we can revisit this idea," are all suitable responses. If the delay goes beyond 60 days and one of us is still not ready, the other must be free to move on. Allowing them to find another partner while you handle your personal issues is the moral and responsible thing to do.

Whether the problem was that I was too busy or didn't have the availability, the reality is that what you're doing is important, but it wasn't a high enough priority for me. So, you need to protect your idea, your investment, and your potential - and just move on. "Go be great!" is how I like to say it. Without any ill will or malicious intent, I choose to free you, and I sincerely hope you accomplish something successful.

If life is happening and I can't commit, I won't waste time holding you back, and you should do the same. Don't hoard opportunities. Be honest and set others free. If I can't give you my best effort and attention because I have too much going on, give me 60 days. If I'm still not ready after that, I need to tell you, as my father would say, "You are free to leave," and wish you total and complete success.

TIP: 5: Daily Commitments

Next in The Business Besties to Business Success is Understanding Daily Commitments. As partners, what daily commitment are we agreeing to? Is it one hour? Two hours? Are we focusing exclusively on this? What are our **daily commitment expectations?**

If our roles and responsibilities are different, and require different levels of time commitment for the interim, we can both understand, but this isn't a reliable long-term solution because fatigue can lead to frustration, and frustration can cause us to react out of character. During the product development phase, your daily commitment might be double mine due to our roles, but that could change once we're underway. I also might be willing to do more now, but please don't assume. We need to discuss what each of us is doing and how we feel about our tasks.

Have a conversation about it.

Remember Ariel from our earlier example? Her partnership failed because she felt overwhelmed and didn't discuss her concerns properly with her business partner. She assumed her partner's relaxed business style meant they weren't committed to success. But what if Ariel was mistaken? What if her partner, the life coach, would have been willing to give more if asked? What opportunities could arise from an honest discussion about their daily commitment?

As you move forward, consider your own daily commitment. If you're handling emails, calls, and marketing all day while I'm focusing on strategy meetings twice a week, resentment could build due to our different roles.

We might not see eye to eye if we don't both value time and manage it differently. For instance, if I don't respond to emails after 7:00 PM, we should discuss this so you understand I'm not ignoring you; my family and our time together are my priority. Every day at 7:00 PM, I stop all work-related activities. If you send me something at 7:11 PM, I probably won't respond until the next day. There may be exceptions, but that's generally my rule. Please understand this in case you need constant feedback and like working late into the night; you might get frustrated working with me because I can't provide instant responses.

I'm not bothered if you see me online on social media. If I've clearly set my availability, I won't ask you work-related questions after hours. If you have one for me, I'll likely address it the next business day. I don't respond to work matters after hours, a point my husband and I still discuss after over 10 years in business together. He's a dedicated worker who might be up working until 2:00 AM on a Saturday, but I'm not reviewing anything sent after business hours. It's not personal; I value your efforts, but I'm prioritizing my time off. That time away allows me to recharge my mind and bring fresh perspectives into the work I do. We've learned that mental breaks matter if you want my best result. So we honor that.

Unless we've agreed to work overnight on a specific project, which happens during big launches, I strictly prefer to work during our business hours. Friend, as you proceed, consider your daily commitments and discuss clear expectations for working hours in your partnership. **It's crucial.**

It's also important to have ongoing weekly meetings for mutual work review. Yes, we met weekly during the expectations and planning phase, but meeting weekly is important for production phases too.

Key questions to ask include: "What did you accomplish?" and "What results did you achieve?" This isn't about showing off, but about building trust and being transparent about everyone's contributions. It helps prevent redundant efforts and ensures we analyze what's driving or hindering revenue. Weekly recaps also maintain project momentum and foster growth.

If I can't meet in person with my partner, I like to send an email on Friday afternoon. It includes a recap of the past week and my plans for the upcoming week. This email serves as a reminder of what I aim to achieve. Even if we haven't spoken by the next Friday, we both know we're making progress toward our goals. The email doesn't need to be lengthy. A simple, "Here's what I've done this week and my plans for next week..." keeps my partner informed about our progress. And I expect the same.

Look, we understand everyone's busy and things are happening fast. Life moves quickly. But if our business plan stays on track, we'll launch on time, without a problem. And if we hit a snag or delay, our effective communication means we can resolve it promptly and professionally.

TIP: 6: Development Budget

Next, we'll discuss something challenging yet crucial: the **estimated development budget**. It's essential to ask upfront, "What will this cost?"

Sometimes, you might partner with someone who has time but lacks financial resources, or vice versa. In such cases, you might contribute more financially based on your potential return on investment. Therefore, it's important to allocate a specific dollar amount accordingly.

When you allocate funds for a project, ensure there's accountability if you're granting others access to those funds. **Don't make assumptions, especially about money.** Review your financial statements and ask questions when needed. If you're covering startup costs for a new venture, it shouldn't include paying for your partner's daily $7 coffee habit. Be proactive and discuss

Personal Accountability Metrics (PAM).

As a business partner, I've learned it's crucial to address small financial missteps early, before they turn into significant mistakes. From my experience, it's often the little things, not the big issues, that can cause problems and lead to bigger challenges.

Address misuse, misunderstandings, and communication issues promptly and effectively, especially concerning finances and spending habits.

You both should have access to log in and review all business and development costs you're expected to cover. If you're sharing project costs, agree on everything upfront. For example, if you want a logo and know someone who charges $250, we might split it at $125 each. Also, I'd want to ensure that we receive three or four design options to choose from and expect a turnaround time of one to two weeks. If these terms work for you, let's proceed and make it happen. Let's both spend the money.

Although, because I can be a bit frugal at times, I might suggest another option: there's a website where we can pay $5 or $10 for excellent logos. I might suggest that we try this option first. It's cheaper and gives us more choices to pick from. Either way, let's discuss how we want to use our funds and which approach will help us get a great logo in the end.

The key is to agree on how we spend money, what it's for, and how much we're spending. If we don't, it can lead to mistrust and uncertainty, which many businesses struggle to overcome.

Let's be open, honest, and completely transparent about money, inviting PAM to discuss. This conversation is essential, vital, and crucial. It's the most important discussion because before making money, there are costs. We need to decide how much we're both willing to invest in this venture and how we'll use that money going forward. This ensures finances won't hinder or distract us from our new business and potential success.

TIP: 7: The Wild-Wild Web...

The online world is like prime commercial real estate. While a domain may cost just a few dollars to acquire, mishandling it could cost thousands more. It's not just about domains, email and social media accounts are also valuable 'property.' Personally, I prefer not to let anyone else own a business domain I'm involved with, except for my husband due to our shared account. In business relationships, controlling the domain means controlling the company. If there's a disagreement, the domain owner holds the power.

I've learned to ensure I either own the domain or share equal access. You can decide how to handle it, but trusting someone blindly isn't wise. Never let anyone exclusively control the domain that represents your business online. Domain registrations come with layers of security, including a primary email, account PIN, and passcode. As a business owner, it's crucial you have equal access to these details.

Not having access to your company's domain is unacceptable.

Even if you feel overwhelmed by technology and don't grasp all the technical details of domain management, ensure it's owned on a shared account, without exception.

If the domain has already been purchased, it should be transferred to a shared account. This is about business, not personal. We need a neutral account accessible to both of us. This ensures fairness, if issues arise later, neither of us has an advantage. You can't take control of the company's domain and disappear without notice. If you try, I'll receive an email alert and can respond. It might seem unnecessary now, but taking these precautions will protect your investment if things ever take a turn.

Email accounts should also be accessible to both parties. When you have a domain, it's important to have professional email accounts and ensure equal access if there's only one primary business email.

Never tie your business's official communications to someone else's personal email account.

Our business shouldn't use my personal Yahoo, Gmail, Outlook, or any other personal email account. All business communications should be directed to our professional email accounts or a neutral email account that we both can access **immediately.**

All communications concerning our company should use that email address, neither theirs nor mine, but the company's email account that we both have unrestricted and unlimited access to.

If you're working with someone who struggles with transparency in your business, that's a major warning sign! It's best to step away. Trust is crucial, and if there's hesitation in being open about communications and email tracking, it's a deal-breaker for me. When there's nothing to hide and no hidden agenda, transparency should come naturally.

If I want to check our email at 7:00 AM to see what's happening, I should have unrestricted access. I shouldn't need to ask for passwords or updates from you, and vice versa. If we're both claiming to run a company together, we both need access to those communications. My name, reputation, and money are all at stake.

It's crucial that everything is clear and fair. When everyone is on the same page, our business has the best chance to succeed. If your potential partner hesitates about full transparency, it's a red flag you shouldn't ignore. Domain ownership and email access should be neutral ground. If they're indifferent or don't have input on domain ownership, it's wise to purchase it yourself to secure your position in the global market. You wouldn't want someone else swooping in and grabbing the domain before either of you does.

TIP 8: Everything shouldn't be free···

One evening, my spouse and I met a guy named Jim in a casual setting. Jim knew beforehand that my husband Wade and I are internet media trainers with experience working with high-profile clients and government agencies. He was eager to learn about our business and explore potential partnerships. However, after meeting Jim, we became uncertain about his dedication to his business. This led us to decide not to collaborate with him.

Jim could have been a promising partner, but his failure to address fundamental business needs made us hesitant to associate our brand, which we've spent ten years building, with his brand.

Jim's fatal business flaws were as follows:

- Jim's email address was not professional. I was not about to copy BiggSexyJ1976@----.com on any business correspondence.

- Jim's website was labeled as a 'free website' filled with intrusive third-party ads. I was genuinely worried that clicking on his 'free' website might infect my computer with a virus!

- Jim's business cards promoted a different company he wasn't associated with and were another 'free' product

For me, that's three strikes and you're out. What Jim didn't understand is that using all those 'free' services signals to clients, partners, and investors that you haven't invested in your business and don't take it seriously enough to spend real money on it. If you won't invest $20 in custom business cards or even $10 a month on a professional website with a professional email, I can't trust your ability to handle a business deal properly.

It also reflects a mindset that often holds back people with great ideas from starting their businesses. **Scarcity is real.**

When you're committed to something and have invested in it, you're less likely to give up when faced with challenges. That's why I always advise my clients to allocate a monthly budget for their business operations, communications, and marketing. Even if it's just fifty or a hundred dollars, it shows the world, and more importantly yourself, that you're serious about your goals.

I believe that if you're not fully committed, like a spoiled child who gets everything without gratitude, you have nothing to lose. This makes partnering with you risky. Either commit wholeheartedly or leave.

Recap I

Okay, let's summarize. We've covered a lot in the first 8 sections of Business Besties, so let's review the key points before moving forward.

- Firstly, set the stage. Ensure the energy, passion, purpose, idea, and concept are all excellent. It's crucial that we, as partners, are aligned.

- Next, set clear expectations. Let's find a win-win solution. How can we make this new business work well for both of us?

- You want to discuss our roles and responsibilities. Specifically, what tasks are you handling and what tasks am I responsible for?

- You're looking to set Personal Accountability Metrics. What do I expect from you, and what do you expect from me? **(Hello PAM!)**

- Next, ensure there's a clear division of tasks and proper time management.

- Next, decide on a realistic timeline for development before launch, considering that unexpected events can affect everyone.

- Discuss the daily commitments as well as initiate weekly recaps.

- Review and come to an agreement on the estimated development costs and total budget.

- Decide on our new business domain and use a professional company email. As partners, we should both have equal access to the domain, email, and website accounts because I want full transparency.

- Lastly, *resist the free!* Respect your vision and business by investing in it. Potential clients might hesitate to work with you if you haven't shown you're committed to funding your dream. Purchase your domain, set up a professional email account, and invest in business cards for about twenty dollars. It makes a real difference. Ask yourself, *"Why should a client invest in my business if I haven't?"*

TIP: 9: Letting your baby grow.

You've invested a lot of time, energy, and effort into your new idea. You feel ready to launch and see it take off. However, there are a few more things I want you to consider. There are still important conversations to have. Here's an important call out: Money might not start flowing in right away. You need to give your idea time to grow. If finances are tight, it can be challenging, but the truth is, it may take time and more investment before your business starts making a profit.

Imagine having a toddler. If I expect my two-year-old to earn money for our family, we'd be homeless and hungry soon. I need to let that baby grow! Similarly, when my child becomes an adult, if I've raised her well, she'll have the skills to create a successful life for herself. Treat your business with the same patience and nurturing.

Friend, you've got to give your business time to develop.

If you're lucky and your business is booming with cash flow, that's great! But it's important to realize that for most people, that's not the usual outcome, even if it's our dream. To see your business succeed, you'll need to give it time to grow, just like raising a child.

In our daily business as developers of online radio stations and podcasts, we offer a product called "Studio in a Box."

It's a complete podcast studio packaged into one. Along with the equipment, clients get access to a training course. We recommend going through this course to learn how to use the equipment effectively. Additionally, we encourage clients to take our online training on sales techniques and schedule a personalized training session with our business development team.

Simply ordering the product isn't enough. If you don't grasp your market and know how to sell to it, you won't maximize your revenue potential. Having potential is good, but making money requires another level of skill. Research and development are crucial, but equally important is learning how to effectively sell to your clients. If selling isn't your strong suit, but your business model depends on it, we've got a challenge to tackle.

TIP: 10: Who's Selling to Whom

If you dislike selling but your business depends on it, now is the time for you and your partners to discuss how we can grow our business and what sales mean for us.

In my world, I never feel like I'm pushing anyone to buy anything. I see it as offering consultations with choices. I won't pressure you into buying. Instead, I provide solutions to your problems and share my knowledge from my education and experience.

After that, what happens next is up to you.

Whether you decide to buy a solution to your problem or not, it's up to you. You can choose to resolve the issue or keep it as is. Either way is fine with me. It's not personal, but recognizing the sales aspect of my business helps me manage expectations effectively.

Recognizing that my sales efforts directly impact my bottom line is crucial. If I avoid selling, it signals to you, my partner, that making money isn't a priority for me. On the other hand, if you're constantly pushing and promoting products while I'm relaxed with my family and not contributing to sales, it can lead to fatigue and frustration. This frustration might cause you to act out of character, and that's something we want to avoid.

We need to discuss our sales strategy for our products. Now that we have this amazing product, how will we promote and sell it? Will you rely solely on promoting it to friends on Facebook, and what's the next step if that doesn't work? Should I expect you to meet a certain quota or bring in a specific number of new clients each month? And if you don't, what does that mean for our future?

If I consistently bring in 20 new clients while you bring in only two, should we still receive equal pay? If not, how will commissions and compensation be determined?

It's crucial to have these conversations before making any sales. Trust me, this situation can arise and you don't want to find yourself in a successful business with a partner who isn't pulling their weight. They might mistakenly think everything is fine because of the positive results, but those results might be solely due to your efforts. If you're not fairly compensated for your efforts, we'll have an issue, *Friend*.

Now, how do you define sales effort and success? We've discussed productivity and development efforts, but what about sales and long-term success? What does successful sales mean for our partnership?

Who sells what, when, and how we are paid, are matters worth a discussion or two⋯

TIP: 11: Advertising & Promotions

Okay, this next section is about advertising and marketing, and it's one of my favorite business subjects.

I'm passionate about advertising and marketing because when you truly believe in what you're doing, it's your responsibility to share it with the world!

You're obligated to not keep it a secret and to present this opportunity to more than just your family and friends.

So, *Friend,* how are we going to promote our new business?

How can we spread the word about this fantastic new sisterhood concept?

Hey, what are your thoughts on using social media for marketing? Are you planning to promote it widely across Facebook, Instagram, and Twitter, or should I not expect that? What's the advertising plan here?

Are we planning to do everything for free, or should we establish some guidelines for our advertising policy and budget?

How you approach your advertising can significantly impact your business. Even with a great product, it's crucial to allocate funds to promote it effectively!

When your advertising is genuine and shares your business story, you can forge a strong connection with your audience and potential customers that could last for years. People invest in the promise of what you offer. They want to believe your product will enhance their lives. Once you create that kind of trust, the price of the product becomes less important. Customers will pay what's needed to achieve their desired results. They're buying into a vision and a solution. Your marketing must address these key elements. **Just do it**, right?

TIP: 12 – Social Media Marketing

One strategy I find effective is online advertising, particularly on YouTube. I value the impact of client testimonials on YouTube they're powerful. To encourage testimonials, I offer promotions and discounts. I ask my clients to share their experiences on camera, knowing I'll use it to attract new business. It's important to be transparent about this.

I'm okay with offering a promotional package where you get a 10 percent discount on our services if you give us a testimonial afterward. However, if my partner has concerns about discounting services for testimonials, we need to discuss it beforehand. It's important to me that we're both on the same page before I make the offer, because I'm representing both of us.

If my partner doesn't see the value in online or social media marketing, we need to align our views. Online and social media marketing often requires patience it's not always an instant success. Sometimes, it takes 30 to 60 days of marketing before seeing results.

I have products that cost over $20,000 each. While they don't sell every day, I allocate a substantial marketing m. When they do sell, it has a significant ct, which is crucial to me.

I also prioritize safeguarding our company's online marketing budget. If funds are needed elsewhere, we won't cut from advertising because it's crucial for generating revenue, especially online. Strategic online marketing boosts our visibility, and it's essential that my business partner and I agree on this approach. If we didn't, it could cause issues.

Here's another example related to business, partnership, and advertising. My partner and I don't always agree on billboard advertising. Personally, I notice billboards, but unless they're very creative and repeated often, I'm not always convinced they're effective. If we have to choose between investing in a billboard campaign or an online social media campaign, I usually prefer social media. However, my partner might prefer the billboard option. In these situations, we need to decide based on what's best for our goals, which sometimes involves compromise. For instance, we might agree to try a billboard for the summer and switch to online advertising in the fall. After both campaigns end, we review their results objectively.

Friend, It's important to stay flexible and remember that in business, agreements and disagreements aren't about being right or wrong. Ego has no place in business—it can lead to problems. No matter the issue, always consider your partner and aim for a win-win solution. Even when you don't agree, find a way for both sides to benefit.

Regarding social media and online marketing, different platforms work differently depending on your product. Some people see great results from Twitter, others from Facebook or Instagram, and some from YouTube. It takes time and patience to figure out which platform works best for you.

If you're not sold on online marketing but your partner is, give them the space to experiment and learn from both successes and failures. This exploration might lead to finding the right strategy that works for your business.

Friend, constantly criticizing something you disagreed with initially won't benefit your business.

I suggest allocating a set timeframe and budget for an online media campaign, billboard campaign, brick-and-mortar campaign, newspaper campaign, etc., and then evaluating the results based on performance.

And that's the key: **results**. You can't argue with results, so test different advertising methods in short trial periods and stick with what works best for you!

When it comes to online advertising, I suggest investing a few hundred dollars per campaign per market. It's a good rule of thumb because if you want something to be effective, you need to allocate sufficient funds to it.

BUSINESS BESTIES

Running a business is always about growth and evaluation. You're continually growing and figuring out what works and what doesn't.

TIP: 13: Internet Marketing

Online marketing is a entirely different world compared to traditional methods. You and your partner need to discuss how you want to engage with Google and SEO.

SEO stands for Search Engine Optimization. It involves choosing the best search terms for your business so that when someone looks them up online, your products or services appear in the search results. Many books and strategies focus on SEO, covering how to select the right keywords and manage your budget to make your company stand out. Mastering this is crucial for success in online marketing!

In today's digital age, as partners, you need to be ready to handle challenging questions and find solutions about your online presence and promotional strategies.

For instance, questions like "Do you need to rank first on Google?" or "Are there other ways to catch our niche market's eye?" As someone with over ten years in social media advertising, I can tell you there are alternatives. Depending on your background, you might think SEO, search engine optimization, is the only route. I've been around long enough to know that's not always true, though outcomes can differ based on what you're selling.

So, *Friend,* what will be your SEO strategy, and what's your SEO budget? Also, what keywords are you going to use for your SEO? Are you planning to hire someone who knows the business to do it for you? Are you going to contact Google directly and take a chance on it yourselves?

Friend, have *that* conversation.

TIP: 14 – Famous Friends

Celebrities and sponsorships are another area we need to consider carefully. Are we going to pursue them, and if yes, who will we choose? From my experience, starting with local celebrities is great when you have a limited budget, because they are often more affordable than big Hollywood names.

A local endorsement can greatly help spread the word about your new business. It's worth researching if there's a local radio host, musician, actor, or community leader who might be interested in trying your products or services in exchange for an interview or promotional opportunity.

When I work or network with celebrities, I always make sure to discuss with my partner how we can make this work best for us.

It's important to discuss what level of sponsorship we feel comfortable providing. We don't want to give away the entire business, so what are we both willing to risk for the chance of celebrity exposure?

Recap II

You're all set to launch. That's fantastic! Now, let's review your marketing steps.

- How are we managing sales, sales outcomes, sales training, and advertising?

- What methods are we using for advertising?

- How long are we planning to run our advertising campaigns?

- What's our policy on sponsorships?

TIP: 15: All About the Benjamins

This next section is crucial. The reason you start a business is to make money, and if you're lucky, you get to do it with your best friends. However, you don't want financial disagreements to strain your friendships. That's why this part of the book about the money conversation is so important.

Friend, You need to be open and honest about your concerns to have this conversation and find a solution that benefits both of you. So, if there are any other personal issues with your partner, it's important to address them before discussing money.

If I'm already feeling resentful towards my friend about something else, anything she says about money will likely be filtered through my defensive mindset.

Honestly, it's the same in any relationship. If my business partner and I are already disagreeing about something, I'll be cautious when she wants to talk about money. We might decide to postpone the budget discussion and focus on resolving our current disagreement first. Or I might need time to gather my thoughts and move past what's bothering me before we discuss finances.

Friend, to have a productive conversation, you need to be clear, open, and ready to listen and understand. Let's approach the topic of money with openness, honesty, and transparency, *without* taking offense. If you and your partner have different financial perspectives, this can feel daunting, but it's important to address openly.

If you have more available resources to spend or have more wealth than your partner in this situation, be sensitive and considerate of their realities and concerns, especially if they're not as financially stable or secure. Be mindful of how your words and tone might affect them. They may not have the same disposable income to invest in the business, but that doesn't make you superior to them. Let's avoid elitism, Friend.

Maybe your money is readily available for use, while they've had to save for six months just to invest $500 in this venture. This might mean they're more cautious about spending because money hasn't come as easily to them as it has to you. Be aware of their situation.

If you're not as financially stable as your partner, try **not** to take offense. Instead, be honest about what you can and cannot afford. It's important to be open and straightforward in these discussions.

If you can't afford something, **say so**. Necessity sparks creativity. If I need a thousand dollars, I'll find creative ways to get it, and you can too. But if I lie about having the money, creativity won't help. So, be honest about your finances. If you can do something, great. If you can't, that's okay too. If you're unsure, that's fine as well - just **communicate openly about it all**, *Friend.*

As partners, this is a crucial part of your journey because I often tell people that how you manage small amounts of money reflects how you'll handle larger sums. The mindset you use for $5, $10, or $100 will apply to $5,000, $10,000, or even $100,000. **Believe me**.

You need to handle the small details correctly. Clear communication is key when you're starting out, especially at the foundational level before the big money comes in.

TIP: 16: Ugh. The Legal Stuff.

Alright, let's get real about money! It's time to have a clear discussion about *finances*. But first, let's go over some legal essentials to ensure you **keep** the money you earn or invest in your business.

If you're starting a new business, you'll need to establish it legally as an LLC, corporation, or similar entity recognized by the government. It's wise to consider hiring a lawyer or using online services like LegalZoom or LegalShield to protect your financial assets thoroughly. Next, you'll need an EIN (Employer Identification Number). This number is like a social security number for your business, ensuring you comply with tax obligations. Many financial institutions require an EIN before offering credit, loans, or banking and insurance services.

When discussing with your business partner, decide on the plan for handling accounting and legal matters. Clarify who will manage each task to ensure our new business is completely legitimate and compliant. If you're not handling the paperwork yourself, remember to follow up on the business's status in a few weeks. You can ask your partner for updates or check your company's status on the Secretary of State's website for your state. Either way, ensure this is addressed promptly to avoid complications later on.

Friends, It's crucial to gather these details because you can't simply decide to do something without legal preparation. Not setting up your business properly can lead to serious consequences. For example, if something goes wrong, you could be sued personally. Without legal protections shielding your personal assets, a lawsuit could seize any assets you own because you haven't established a clear separation between yourself and the business. It's essential to formally establish your business as its own entity by filing with your state.

Know that there are upsides and downsides to everything, and I won't give direct advice since I'm not a tax attorney. However, with over 20 years in business, I can say from experience that having that separation is crucial. It's like a security blanket for your business and it's just the smart move.

TIP: 17: Who's Got Bank

The next important discussion after sorting out the legalities is to talk openly about bank accounts. Are you planning to set up a business account? If so, who will provide the funding, and where will it come from? Whose name will be on the accounts, and are there any concerns about that?

Here's a real-life story for you. Two friends wanted to start a consulting company together. One of them, Tammy, was a single mom with a full-time job and limited funds to invest. However, she had time to develop the website, gather content crucial for it, and manage social media. The other friend, Jessica, was married and financially well-off. She decided to fund their shared dream personally for six months.

When they tried to open a bank account for the business, they faced a hiccup. It turned out Jessica's husband was the one putting $10,000 into the venture. Because of this, he insisted on being listed on the account, even though he wasn't part of their business plan. This created a complication they hadn't anticipated.

Jessica's husband proposed splitting the business ownership into thirds, giving him and Jessica a larger share. Tammy was taken aback by this suggestion. Instead of agreeing to the new terms right away, she chose to put the business on hold until they could have more talks about how ownership would be divided.

The two women and Jessica's husband returned to discussing their business idea. Jessica and Tammy needed to decide whether they would accept financial support from a third party, even if it's from a spouse. Moreover, with Jessica's husband financing the business and Tammy handling all the operational work, they had to clarify Jessica's contribution. What unique value was she bringing to the venture? They needed to answer these questions and more before making any decisions to proceed.

My take: If you're giving me a $10,000 check to support my business, that's great—just hand over the money without conditions. But if you're making an investment and want to be a silent partner, we'll need to document that agreement. As main partners, we must agree on these terms before I accept any money from you.

In this situation, Tammy, the single mom, felt uneasy about Jessica's husband being on the business bank account. She believed it would create a situation where it was two against one. Even though he was supposed to be a silent partner, she anticipated he would have opinions and she didn't want his input in their new business. As a result, they decided not to partner for this venture and chose to pursue separate paths instead. They left open the possibility of revisiting the idea in a year or two.

After a while, Tammy changed her mind about the situation. She realized that if it only took $10,000 to make it work, she could raise that amount in two years. So, when they talk about it again, if Jessica's husband still plans to put in $10,000, Tammy will have her $10,000 ready too. With a bigger budget, they might achieve even more. However, she made it clear that she wouldn't give up her voice, authority, or control over the business finances, no matter what.

I really like this example because it shows that managing money is crucial. Your attitude toward getting funds from silent partners or third parties is also important.

Set up the bank account in the business's name but be clear about who's in control. Is it me and the partner, or is it me, the partner, the partner's spouse, and her mother-in-law because she gave some money too? I ask this because if you let everyone who contributes money get involved, things could get messy fast if they think their dollar buys them a voice or control in your new business.

Friend, **before** you're at the bank, ready to sign and deposit someone's investment, make sure you've been very clear about everyone's roles and that everyone agrees. Speaking of agreements, make sure it's properly and legally documented. As they say, Friend, show me the **contract!**

TIP: 18: I'm Watching You

Next, let's discuss something we've mentioned before: accountability in spending. In some partnerships, it works best when two people must authorize any payment over a certain dollar amount.

Friend, Did you know you can arrange your bank account to do that?

Some partnerships function better with an honor system where I trust you to act responsibly. If I have any questions, I have access to all information. For example, if I check our shared online business banking account and see a $25 charge at Starbucks, I might ask, "What was this $25 at Starbucks from the joint account for?" And you might respond, "Oh, I had a consulting meeting with our web designer and covered the bill for our meeting and working lunch."

Now that I understand from your explanation, I'm like, "Oh, okay, cool.

However, if I ask you about the $25 Starbucks transaction and you get offended, you might not be mature enough for business.

Friend, You have to understand that people can't read your mind. If they weren't there and don't understand what you did, it's crucial to explain it confidently without feeling threatened. **It's really important**. You need to be able to explain yourself without feeling attacked. If you get offended, to me, it means you might have something to hide. Your reaction will make me either investigate more or let it go, but I'll remember it, whether I say it out loud or not.

I have a saying in my home that applies to this situation. Especially when raising teenagers, my general rule of thumb is that 1 + 1 should always equal 2. If it doesn't, then something is wrong or has changed in the equation. Either I don't have all the facts, or the facts have changed. Either way, I am on the prowl like a cat, ready to solve the mystery.

Maybe you've done something you shouldn't have, and your conscience is making you overreact to my simple question. Your unclear response creates confusion. In business, accountability checks are important, and ensuring everyone has the same information is crucial for long-term success.

It's also important to be able to ask questions for clarification or when you don't understand something, without causing offense.

If I ask a question and my tone seems accusatory or suspicious, it shows I don't trust my partner, which might mean I'm not ready for this business venture. Maybe I need to take a step back because my lack of trust could be my issue, not yours. It could be because in a past partnership, someone let me down and broke my trust, making it hard for me to trust anyone now.

That history of deception may come out through my tone when I speak to you.

Maybe it's just a gut feeling, but I don't trust you. Either way, I need to ensure my tone is neutral or friendly when asking about finances. If not approached properly, something simple can easily turn negative.

TIP: 19: The Money Tree

Friend, Next, let's talk about recurring revenue options. I really like this because it ensures we have a way to consistently generate income in our business model. We should ask each other questions such as:

* How are we going to keep growing beyond the initial launch?

* What is our game plan for ongoing success?

* Do we have a strategy to generate additional capital?

This meeting is where you brainstorm additional ways to generate revenue. You might want to discuss topics such as:

* Can we add a subscription service to what we're doing?

*Can we add long term coaching or consulting to what we're doing?

* Can we add a quarterly check in to what we're doing?

* What are the options here to create monthly recurring revenue?

* Is there a possibility for a monthly service fee that we can incorporate into the business model?

And so forth and so on...

I strongly believe it's crucial to include a recurring revenue model in your business plan. Over the past twenty years, I've consulted with various businesses beauty salons, health and wellness firms, travel agencies, even government entities and each time, I've recommended incorporating a monthly recurring revenue model. If you're unsure how to do this, feel free to reach out to someone like me with experience who can guide you through the process.

I think every successful business model includes some form of monthly recurring revenue. Every business aims for repeat customers. The key is identifying the right service or product and ensuring customers keep coming back for more.

Friend, Sometimes, it requires creativity and thinking outside the box a bit, but it's possible. McDonald's constantly airs commercials, runs promotions, offers specialty items, and even hosts giveaway games for a reason their business model isn't just about selling burgers once, but about bringing you back again and again to buy burgers from them.

For more details or to schedule a one-on-one marketing call about available monthly recurring revenue options for your industry, visit www.PinkroseMarketing.com

(Okay, now that that shameless plug for Pinkrose Marketing LLC, is over let's get back to the book!)

TIP: 20: Call My Lawyer!

Next, let's talk about legal liabilities. It's crucial to plan ahead for what we'll do if things don't go as expected despite our brilliant strategy.

This discussion should tackle things such as:

- What happens when/if it all goes wrong?
- Who's at fault?
- How will we manage disagreements, customer issues, and complaints?
- Do we have a strategy for resolving issues, or are we going to criticize the customer (or each other) and move on?
- Are we going to ignore problematic customers?
- Are we going to have an actual dispute or company complaint policy?
- If you provide a service as my partner and it's faulty, how will we address that?
- What happens if we get sued?
- What is our legal game plan?

I hope you see my point, because not every day in business will be a huge success. There will be setbacks along the way, and how we handle these challenges will determine how long our business partnership lasts.

Friend, Let's discuss liabilities, because ignoring them can jeopardize your business success. My point here again, is not to solve legal liabilities and its related issues for you, but to encourage and advise you to tackle the legal questions head on WITH a legal professional.

TIP: 21: Customer Disputes

I'm currently consulting with a client and have seen similar situations before with unique business models. Let's call my client Rebecca. She has a fantastic concept that's gaining popularity quickly. However, because Rebecca wasn't ready for such rapid growth, she's now dealing with the consequences of being unprepared.

Rebecca is in full panic mode right now. Negative customer reviews about her company's customer service are damaging her online reputation. Despite her innovative and impressive product, which should be catching the eye of major retailers, it's now facing harsh criticism and ridicule on the same social media platforms that initially boosted its popularity.

The situation has become severe for Rebecca's company. They can't share a picture, tweet, or post a Facebook posts without customers' complaints flooding the comments. As a consumer or potential customer, this negative activity would deter me from doing business with her company.

Like most buyers, before I buy anything online, I do research. If I visit your company's social media and see complaints about unanswered emails and bad experiences, I won't spend any money with you.

Many people posted online that Rebecca's company wasn't answering phone calls and had poor customer service. Knowing Rebecca personally, I knew she was a good person, but unfortunately, her company couldn't deliver as quickly as promised. Customers were rightly upset about the delays in product delivery.

Rebecca's partners had left her in charge of daily operations without fully understanding the challenges she faced. After a few consultations, I encouraged her to hold a meeting and update the entire team everyone from employees to management about the situation.

Initially, Rebecca hesitated to share because she believed she could handle everything alone. Trusting my instincts and experience, I urged her to inform everyone about the seriousness of the situation, so she could move forward honestly, and eventually she did. During this crucial meeting with her team, Rebecca explained to staff and investors that a key vendor had failed them, preventing them from fulfilling customer orders as promised.

Rebecca finally did something I had been advising her to do all along: she set aside her pride and asked her team for help.

Many team members had seen the social media complaints and knew the company was struggling.

However, because Rebecca hadn't addressed it with them, they didn't feel comfortable discussing the situation or offering solutions. They also didn't know how to bring up what they were seeing. Now that Rebecca had called the meeting, her team felt free to speak openly about their experiences. Many of them had great ideas on how to handle the vendor issues and turn the situation around.

Customer disputes can ruin your business if you don't manage them. I don't always believe the customer is always right. I believe in what's right, so if someone complains about my business or service, I want to know. I'm not too busy proving you wrong to hear or accept criticism. But once you've shared your grievances, if there are valid responses, I'll provide them.

This is especially true when dealing with entrepreneurs because sometimes they're facing their own fears and insecurities about their new business venture. Not all, but a few new business owners are not mentally or financially ready to face the challenges that come with launching a new business or service. It's easier for them to blame someone else for their lack of results than to admit their own shortcomings such as, *"I didn't follow the training procedure"*.

TIP: 22: Client Accessibility

One of our biggest challenges as a company happened a couple of years ago when we switched our customer service model. Before, if you called between 10:00 AM and 7:00 PM, you would speak to my partner, myself, or one of our admins. Someone was always answering the phones, no matter what your issue was. We were always just a phone call away.

Then we realized we were spending hours every day on customer service training and answering the same questions over and over again. So, we decided there had to be a better use of our time. We implemented a new customer service policy and procedure for technical support issues.

Now, if you're calling our company for sales, we can definitely get someone to speak with you because you may need clarification to make a purchase. But if you are a current client calling about a training issue, we'll direct you to where that information is easily available and accessible online.

Also, I'm not going to hold your hand while you read or watch a video. If you need extra help beyond the online resources, we implemented a ticket system for additional contact and 24/7 support from our technical team. It won't be immediate or by phone, but it will be thorough. No one will get lost in the land of never returned calls or emails ever again.

Although it was a great idea to help us become more pragmatic, this change was initially very problematic. Our client list was in the hundreds, and if everyone called because they couldn't figure out something simple, we would lose a lot of time. It was very time-consuming and kept us from gaining new sales.

Initially, we lost customers when we shifted to an online service model for technical support. We were surprised by how some customers expected us to act as their personal servants just because they bought a service from us. We received complaints simply because they couldn't speak to me whenever they wanted! **It was mind blowing.**

I remember one client who was very upset that she couldn't get me to change something for her, even though she could do it herself. She was rude and aggressive towards me and my staff. I wanted to tell her, "Hey, the information is still available online, which should be faster for you than waiting two or three days for me to call you back." But she wasn't interested. We even brought in new members of our training team who were highly qualified and knowledgeable. But for some people, that still wasn't enough. They insisted on speaking directly to me or my managing partner. Why? Because they wanted personalized attention and didn't want to follow the proper procedure.

You need to be careful when dealing with clients who have become overly familiar with you.

At first, I used to take calls like that, but I learned to be strategic. Instead of answering your question directly, let me explain why we've updated our support services model. We're traveling more for trainings, which limits our availability. Also, our admin isn't equipped for technical support, so calling her is a waste of time if she can't assist you. However, our new online training tutorial support center has nearly thirty training videos on that exact issue and more. If you can't find the topic in a video, you can email our support team. They'll either create a new video for you or send a step-by-step email guide.

We also needed a way to track and be accountable. I want you to know that your call won't be missed and your issue will be resolved. You might tell me you called and left a message, while my admin says she doesn't know about it. By submitting a support ticket, it gives us accountability. We can see who had an issue, who will handle it, and track how quickly we resolve it.

Once I explained to our current clients that this change was necessary for us to improve our service to them, they understood. They weren't upset anymore about not being able to call for technical support directly. Now, they all use the technical support system without any problems. Many even like the tracking system because they can look back and find answers to questions they had asked months ago. They can log into their account and see their history, getting the same answer again without interrupting my training sessions.

Here's my point: You need to have a game plan in place. Consider your options for customer support and technical assistance.

Friend, Don't assume you won't encounter customer support issues because you will. Every business does. But what really sets apart great customer service from poor service is how companies respond to these issues.

Create a strategy with your business partner now. This plan will allow you to expand your business while also retaining existing clients and accounts. By planning for maximum capacity, you'll establish a foundation to consistently exceed your customers' expectations.

TIP: 23: The Truth About Taxes

Let's discuss taxes for a moment. My advice is straightforward: PAY THEM. Make sure to hire a tax attorney and avoid using a casual or unqualified tax preparer through personal connections. It's best to seek professional and competent tax assistance through proper channels.

I believe it's crucial to hire impartial professionals. Even if your cousin is a certified CPA, which is great for them, when you're in a partnership and your business includes someone who isn't family, it's important to find a neutral professional to handle your accounting and taxes.

I started this book with a personal example about my sister. A real reality is that when my sister calls me for business advice, I prioritize her interests over her partner's. This isn't a criticism of me; it's actually about protecting my sister. Since she's closest to me, I always advise what's best for her.

If she says, 'Hey, we want to do something···' I'll consider the risks or liabilities she might face. What potential problems could she be opening herself up to? What issues might she not have thought about, and advise her accordingly.

BUSINESS BESTIES

While I excel in my own work, I'm not the ideal person to advise my sister on her business partnerships because my perspective is biased towards her. I'm always going to prioritize her interests, and not remain neutral. It's best to seek advice from someone without that personal bias, who can offer fair and practical guidance that benefits **both** of you equally. Look for impartial experts for neutral advice.

If you're not my sister, we're good. I can share everything, open up about my 20 years of business experience without hesitation. But when it's family, I prioritize their well-being, so my advice might not be the best for *you*. Remember, everyone is human. No matter how professional they are, we're all human—maybe like superheroes, but still human, Friend.

I'll always prioritize my own or my family's interests first. You should expect the same from your family. That's why it's crucial to seek impartial experts for services like accounting, taxes, CPA, and insurance in a partnership.

Don't go with the home girl hookup.

Pay the full price. It's important to compensate people fairly for their services, knowledge, and expertise. I don't want my business to be undervalued in this regard, and I believe in mutual respect. I'll pay for your work, and I expect the same in return for mine.

We show a lack of values when we seek discounts on important things, yet splurge on full-priced designer styles and fashions that aren't essential.

When you hire a professional, you're expecting their best. So, Friend, go find the best accountant your money can buy!

TIP: 24: The Right Way to Quit

Friend, let's talk about what happens if this doesn't work out.

People say love and hate are closely related, and I think it's because they both involve intense energy. The difference lies in how you interpret that energy based on your own experiences.

At the start of this business venture, we had no experience just hope and excitement. But now, I'm seeing that you're not committed and your work is sloppy, and it's hurting my brand. My recent experiences with you are telling me I need to leave quickly and without a clear separation plan, things could get messy and unpleasant.

It can be challenging to stay professional when emotions are in play. To prevent complications, let's create a separation plan in advance. This ensures we're both clear about the process in case feelings change. Similar to prenuptial agreements in marriages, this plan clarifies that if certain conditions aren't met, we'll dissolve our legal commitment and go separate ways. If separation becomes necessary, here's our agreed approach.

Prenuptial agreements are common in marriages, yet they're often overlooked in business contexts. I propose considering one. It doesn't need to be overly complex, just a clear guideline. For instance, if we decide to dissolve our business, we'll share the dissolution costs. We agree to stop using the business name and promoting it. We also commit to a six-month break before starting a similar venture.

Specify how clients are managed and retained: Who, How, Where, When, and How Often are crucial points. Knowing what happens to your client base, which the business relies on, is vital. These terms must be agreed upon before launching your business. Avoid potential problems down the road by having these discussions or formalizing them in a legal contract.

Friend, I've seen a situation where two people started a business together, but then decided to part ways. The very next day, the person who had all the website information, images, content, and access to the client base started a new company with someone else!

You would and should feel betrayed, knowing how hard you worked to get things going. But if you didn't have any separation agreement, they have the right to start a new business, take your name off the door, and move on.

It's important to have these tough and uncomfortable conversations early on. If we decide to part ways, what will the procedure be? What is expected of me? What is expected of you? If the rules are clear, there's no need for a lot of extra emotion or angry theatrics!

TIP: 25: Code of Conduct

I tell my kids and most of them are now nearing or at adulthood that at the start of each school year, we put up a poster in the main hallway with the house rules. My husband and I were intentional about making our expectations and guidelines clear.

For example, if you were in elementary school, bedtime was 9:30 pm. For middle school, it was 10:30 pm, and for high school, you had to be in your room by 11:30 pm. Also, elementary students had to unplug from technology at least 30 minutes before bedtime, and the same rule applied to middle and high school students.

Now, let's talk about grades. If your grades fell below 80, you would miss out on the honor roll, which was a big deal in our house. But if you were failing a subject, you were completely shut down - no technology, no cell phone, no social media, no hanging out with friends, and *no exceptions.*

Failing was not an option that got a passive response from us as parents. If you chose to fail, knowing you were smart enough to do the work and capable of learning, you were choosing to accept those consequences.

Before you judge our strictness, let me explain how things worked in the Lester Dunn household. Yes, we were serious about failing, but we were even more serious about good grades. If someone got all A's and B's, we'd check them out of school in the middle of the day and take them to a restaurant of their choice for an honor roll lunch. We'd then post pictures of our grinning student enjoying a well-deserved dessert on social media.

As a family, we always emphasized the positive, but occasionally someone would bring home a bad grade. When this happened, because they knew our expectations, they'd hand over their cell phone as soon as they walked in the door from school.

If one of my sons got a bad grade, they'd go to their room and hand over their game controller. There was no yelling, arguing, or drama. The consequences of not meeting expectations were clear on a poster we passed every day. This approach also helped my husband and me maintain fairness and prevent manipulation in our blended family home.

Everyone understood the rules, and we all knew the consequences. There was no point in trying to pit one parent against the other, as our house rules were clear and posted for everyone to see. Both the kids who struggled and those who excelled understood them perfectly well.

Interestingly, it's similar in business. You need clear expectations and consequences. Without a code of conduct or ethical behavior, or if we take risky actions leading to company dissolution, we face the consequences. Knowing these upfront lets us proceed logically and confidently.

It's something you hope you never need, but I'd rather you have it and not need it than need it and not have it.

Your business must have a clear code of conduct and shared ethics ingrained in you, your partner, and any future employees. If there are boundaries you won't compromise on, clearly outline the consequences and potential risks if someone steps over the line.

7 Core Business Values

Congratulations! You've completed the most challenging part of this book! If you've had the conversations suggested here with your business partner, you're well on your way to a positive business experience. Before I let you go to enjoy endless business bliss, there are a few important things I want to share with you.

This bonus section of the book introduces my 7 Core Business Values. These aren't just filler content; they're principles that have personally guided me through different business environments over the years. Through my career, I've found these seven values to be crucial. They significantly influence overall business success and how you feel about your decisions, regardless of the business outcomes.

These 7 **Core Business Values** are more than just partnerships. They're personal, and whether you succeed in business depends a lot on how you practice them.

Friend, I can't leave this out of the Friend's Business Guide because you need it, your partner needs it, and honestly, I still need it too. So, let's dive in and start with the first Core Value, which, for me, is integrity.

Core Business Value I - Intergrity

I need to trust that you speak the truth. As my partner, your words should carry weight and consistency, not being insincere or inconsistent. Being flighty means saying one thing to me with one meaning, then referencing the same topic differently when I'm not around.

You might say the right words, but changing their meaning alters their context completely. CYB (Covering Your Behind) might seem sneaky, but for me, meaningful words are honest and consistent, no matter who's listening. Being truthful, especially when it's tough, shows your true character. It's a reflection of your CORE values.

I believe that my honesty reflects who I am as a person, and I make sure to apply this honesty in all my business dealings, no matter the environment. Friend, I'm not saying you can't use tact or wisdom. I understand that sometimes you need to say something in different ways to different people so they can understand it better. However, as long as everyone walks away with the same basic understanding, you've been honest. Your words don't have to be exactly the same every time. It's important to adjust your words depending on the audience to ensure clarity, understanding, and consistency.

Repeating myself doesn't mean I'm being effective. If I can't say the same thing to different audiences with the same meaning, there's an honesty and integrity problem. Friend, at that point, I'm being misleading, and not being completely honest and not having full integrity is a deal breaker for me. I need to know your words have substance and are true, and you should expect the same from me. That's what honesty and integrity are all about. Operating with full truth and transparency matters to me, and it's a core value.

Another aspect of integrity for me is speaking up for what's right. I understand that in today's politically charged climate, "what's right" can vary for different people based on factors like background, upbringing, and demographics. I get that, but at the core, some things are just right and some things are just wrong.

Friend, If I wouldn't want something in the news to happen to me, my children, my parents, or my spouse, then I shouldn't be okay with it happening to others.

Speaking up for what's right and against what's wrong is part of character and integrity. I don't want a partner who sees something wrong and is dismissive or complacent. That's a deal breaker for me. I need you to care about what's happening in the world, to show interest and empathy beyond our business. I don't want partners who dismiss the struggles of communities of color or people different from us. Friend, I can't work with that because if I become unacceptable to you, who's to say you'll continue to accept me? Maybe you'll dismiss my children. Who knows? Either way, I don't want to put that kind of energy into the world, and I don't want to partner with that negativity. A lack of concern for others is a deal breaker.

Additionally, someone who is complacent about wrong things and someone who won't advocate for what's right are the same. If you have a voice or influence, don't just use it for personal gain. Speaking up for those who have no voice is part of integrity and a core business value. It matters.

Core Business Value II: Self-Discipline

Another core business value is self-discipline. Yes, Friend, self-discipline, or as I like to say, "the ability to manage oneself.

Can you resist binge-watching TV or the latest Netflix release when we have a deadline?

Will you have enough self-control to finish the work when motivation fades, or will our business suffer due to your latest interests?

Do you have enough willpower to work through issues?

Do you dismiss them without resolution?

Do you create a mess and then leave it for someone else to deal with?

When it's time to burn the midnight oil are you going to do it?

If this is a moment where we need self-control, *Friend,* do you have it?

If the bank grants us a $25,000 credit line, will you use it responsibly for the business or spend it on unnecessary things? **Self-discipline** is crucial in business it separates success from failure. Countless opportunities have been lost due to lack of discipline. **Let's ensure we don't fall into that trap.**

Michelle was well-known in our online marketing group chat for always sharing insights on the latest industry news. When the American government released billions in small business loans during an economic crisis, many entrepreneurs, including Michelle, applied for them.

After her loan was approved and the funds arrived, she proudly shared in the group about planning a long vacation and making home repairs. While both were important, they weren't directly related to her business's success. After a few weeks, members noticed Michelle hadn't been as active in the group. It seemed like she had vanished.

Later that day, a mutual friend sent me a private message, revealing that Michelle had run into legal trouble for misusing her government loan funds.

They could track how the loans were spent, and they determined that renovating her master bedroom wasn't a necessary business expense. Fortunately, Michelle didn't have a business partner, so her choices didn't affect anyone else directly. However, I don't think she suddenly decided overnight to act dishonestly.

I think there were many small decisions that made her feel untouchable, which wasn't true. With no one to keep her in check, she did as she pleased. Eventually, her lack of self-control led to her company failing. She disappeared from social media and even left town, ashamed and facing legal trouble.

It's often more challenging than people realize to control your thoughts and actions effectively. We frequently struggle with personal habits and spending behaviors that we might not notice because they've never been questioned.

In a co-dependent relationship, foreseeing and preventing potential issues can be crucial for your business to succeed. If your history has taught you to only be accountable to yourself as an adult, self-discipline might pose a challenge. It's not about wrongdoing, but rather about accepting others' opinions and adjusting behaviors to find common ground an aspect of self-discipline often underestimated.

We're aware that overspending can be a problem. If you and your partner disagree on a business purchase, it requires self-discipline to hold off, even if you think it's best for the business. From my experience, making a purchase without agreement can seriously harm your relationship with your partner and make the deal a regrettable one.

Sometimes, you have to let go of things for the greater good and trust that if it's meant for you, it will return. Hopefully, next time, you and your partner can agree on how to proceed. Having the discipline to walk away from opportunities is crucial in a partnership.

Now, the question is, "Can you deny your needs or wants to keep peace and harmony with your partner?"

If you can do this, I encourage you to keep going. But if you truly cannot, then you may not be ready for any form of partnership.

This is especially true for business *and marriage*.

A key part of keeping agreement flowing is knowing when to let go for the greater good. It requires maturity to consistently aim for a win-win situation.

Egos can be destructive in relationships. They lead to fights over being right instead of seeking peace.

Some believe success requires a yin-yang partnership, but I disagree. Harmonious collaboration allows ideas to flow effortlessly. Creative sessions become chances for growth as energy aligns through shared thoughts and insights.

"When you're free from conflict, stubbornness, or pride, you can unleash your best strategies, and that's when the magic happens, Friend.

It's about how you present yourself, and arriving with self-discipline keeps the positives in and the negatives out.

Core Business Value III: Freedom of Thought

In a business environment, I believe every idea deserves respect. If you're willing to share it publicly or in a group, you deserve a respectful audience

There are no bad ideas.

Some ideas may not be ideal for the moment, but I believe there are no bad ideas. In my workplace, I value creativity and freedom of thought for everyone.

I once worked with someone whose title was Chief Thought Producer. I really liked this because it felt like his role was to spark innovation. He would encourage, challenge, and draw out more ideas from you.

He would say, "Hey, here's the problem. Now let's get creative and come up with solutions. Oh! And not just one solution. No, no, no. Let's come up with four or five! Let's think of as many solutions as we can, and then we'll choose the best one for our business together."

He was truly a **Chief Thought Producer**. I've never seen that title before or since, but I loved it. I try to bring that same freedom into my work environments today.

There are times when collaboration isn't possible, and as a CEO or Marketing Director, I have to make the final decision. But whenever we can brainstorm as a group, I'm all in.

I believe that in the best work environments creativity reigns supreme. There must be freedom of thought. Everyone's idea is valid. It might not be the perfect solution right now, but I won't dismiss or diminish you for suggesting it.

I appreciate you. In fact, give me another idea, because guess what? That next one might be the solution we're looking for.

Core Business Value IV: Consideration

Another core business value is **consideration**.

I hope that in our partnership, you'll consider me, and I'll do the same for you. If I'm having a bad day, I need you to be thoughtful, and I'll be considerate of you if you're going through something personal.

I won't badger you or make you feel worse than you already do.

As your partner, I genuinely care about your wellbeing. How you feel matters to me. As a company, we want a culture that cares about your birthday, your health, your family, and any challenges you face. We don't want to be so politically correct that we can't be compassionate.

We want to be in a partnership that celebrates your successes, even if they're not strictly business-related. I've guided my life by the belief that consideration, empathy, and thoughtfulness are core values in business.

Recently, I learned that one of my clients had cancer. I had spent several days with her and her family over the past year and had come to know them well. Hearing about her cancer diagnosis broke my heart. I immediately called and emailed her to let her know I was there for her. As someone who believes in faith, I assured her of my prayers for her full recovery.

I didn't reach out to her with any upsell or new service opportunity in mind. I simply wanted her to know that she was in my thoughts and prayers.

That kind of consideration matters.

Did I have to do it? No. But should I do it? Yes.

When people know they're more than just a customer number or a client file to you, it changes how they feel about you.

Fortunately, my client recovered and was able to resume her company without any lasting negative effects from her time away battling her illness.

Letting people know they matter is a core value, and showing consideration goes a long way, especially when the roles are reversed.

Core Business Value V: Community Success

Another core business value we must address is community success and collaboration. While individual success and recognition are important, the overarching idea of community success is that when we work together as a team, we all succeed together.

When I acknowledge someone on my team, I don't stop there. I know they didn't achieve success alone. It took other thoughts, conversations, and ideas that contributed to the company's success. That's why it's a team effort and a team success. We all share the recognition and potential bonuses.

We're all going on the trip, and we're all going to enjoy ourselves. When you create a culture of team success and fairness in your business by avoiding favoritism and actively recognizing everyone you'll see your staff thrive with a collaborative mindset. It's not me versus you; the best results come when it's me and you together.

Core Business Value VI: Transparency & Authenticity

Next, let's review transparency and authenticity as core values in our business.

I never want anyone I work with to feel they have to hide behind someone else. I don't want anyone to feel they need to hold back or not give their all. In fact, I encourage the opposite. Show me more of who you are. Share your thoughts and energy, because when you give it your all, that's where true success lies.

It's only when everyone can fully be themselves authentically that the magic of business synergy happens. That's where our company always achieves its best results. I truly believe in the importance of transparency and authenticity. I don't need another Koddi; I've got her covered. I need you to be the best version of yourself. Brianna, be the best Brianna. Julie, be the best Julie. Samantha, Shelia, whoever you are, show up fully every day so we can achieve the best possible results.

Core Business Values VII: Respect

Finally, the last business core value we'll discuss is respect. I believe everyone deserves respect, whether you're the janitor or the CEO, **everybody deserves respect.**

I don't tolerate mistreatment of people. Disrespect is something I take seriously and won't accept. "Everyone starts at 100% with me, no matter who you are. I won't let someone else's experience with you change that," Patricia Tubbs, my mentor and former director at IBM (Sports and Technology Marketing), taught me early in my career, and it's something I've always remembered.

If someone has an issue with you, I'll listen out of respect for their experience and try to understand their perspective. However, as my mentor says, "Everyone starts at 100% with me, and based on your actions, you'll either go up or down."

When there's a conflict or grievance, I genuinely try to see things from everyone's perspective. I often bring up viewpoints that hadn't been considered before in tough situations. Keeping a mindset of mutual respect ensures fairness. Even if I don't agree with your position in the end, I hope you feel heard.

It's never okay to belittle someone for having a different perspective. Learning to agree to disagree is important in business; it helps you move past disagreements with mutual respect, allowing for growth.

In today's business and social settings, minor disagreements have become more personal and toxic.

"I find nothing more disappointing than when someone resorts to petty attacks just because we disagree. My motto is simple: 'Stay constructive, not petty!'"

Recap: Core Business Values

These are the fundamental **7 Business Core Values** that I believe in, which have contributed to my long-term and ongoing success.

I believe that integrating these values into your identity as a business partner and owner will lead to enduring and profitable results throughout your entrepreneurial journey.

The Final Warning:

Thank you for the reset.

You know, even professionals can make mistakes. I'm writing the conclusion to this book months after finishing the original manuscript. The delay felt more like a nudge, almost like a higher calling telling me to 'wait a little while, child.' So, I did, and in the meantime, I started a few other business projects some with people I know, and a few on my own.

Then I made one of the biggest mistakes an entrepreneur could make! I started consulting with someone about a new business venture, involving them in my thinking and acknowledging (though not implementing) their ideas, without having a crucial conversation about their commitment.

Because of this, just before my new product was set to launch literally, the order was with the fulfillment vendor everything went wrong. I received a text message that went something like this...

"Hey, we never talked about the organizational structure of this new product line," they said.

"Um, yeah, it's part of my marketing brand. I'm excited to see it come to life!" I replied.

"So, what's my ownership part in this?" – They asked.

"Nothing." My response was straightforward. I could sense some pushback coming, so I added, "I'm using my own money to launch this. The idea and marketing strategy are all mine. Why would you think you deserve an ownership stake just because I ran a few ideas by you? That doesn't make any sense."

At this they became infuriated with me.

They bombarded me with name-calling, character attacks, and insults about who I am. They accused me of being misleading, sneaky, and evil. They acted like I had planned to take advantage of them and run off with the profits from a project that hadn't even started. I let them continue their verbal attack without responding.

I knew it was my fault. I hadn't considered *my* potential from *their* perspective. Blinded by my own excitement, I let them believe in my dream without formally asking them to join me.

There was no recovery, and I knew I couldn't do anything about it. The project was lost. The pure energy and enthusiasm were ruined, and there was no way it could move forward as it was.

To move past the moment and find peace, I offered them an ownership percentage. But anything less than half wouldn't be enough.

Ego was now involved.

Disheartened. Upset. Heartbroken. I ended the conversation with them and started contacting my fulfillment vendors to cancel the parts that were already in motion. This project would have to be altered to remove any aspects that could be credited to them, which meant immediately stopping the order and having everything redone. I didn't want to risk all of my hard work being called into question by a lawyer later, because I allowed a "friend" in on collaboration.

My product in its original form was now a failure, and I took full responsibility. Could I have continued on without changing it? Sure. But would my success be forever tainted? Definitely. In that moment it was clear that because I had not handled my business affairs appropriately, my new project as I originally designed itg was now a no-go. I wouldn't be able to continue on with my plans as I had envisioned them, and the joy of this new venture was forever tainted.

Navigating friendship and business requires caution. Offering genuine joy, helpful advice, or assistance can lead others to believe they deserve a share of your work, especially if you use their suggestions or talents. Using someone as a sounding board cost me my entire dream. Casual conversations over lunch and brunch made them feel entitled to ownership, despite not contributing anything tangible.

I often tell clients, "Free help usually comes with strings attached." It's crucial to clarify terms upfront before enthusiasm leads to unexpected complications.

I understand why they wanted to join a project with significant income potential. Their insistence on ownership suggests the concept's validity and likely strong market appeal. However, I made a mistake in interpreting their interest as a gesture of goodwill.

As I sit here now, making adjustments to everything I had planned, the costs of changing concepts, designs, and methods are adding up. I have no one to blame but myself. As an expert, I didn't follow my own advice, and now I'm facing the consequences. **This one really stings**.

Hopefully, my experience can benefit you. Remember this story when discussing your new idea with your best friend. Before asking them about details like "Yellow or Blue

Bottles?" or "Script or Block lettering?", first clarify if they are willing to be an advisor and what they expect in return. Each conversation could lead to them claiming a share of your company, which you should know from the start.

I regret opening up and sharing my ideas with someone I believed genuinely supported my success, not seeking personal benefit. Now, having to revisit every conversation, even those where I sought their input, to ensure they didn't influence my decisions is frustrating. Their suggestions didn't align with my vision, but to avoid being rude, I repeatedly redirected the conversation to stay true to my original plan. Yet, in their view, they believe they contributed to my success.

Could I have done it alone? Absolutely. So why did I seek advice or a "sounding board" in the first place, you wonder? Well, the answer is straightforward. I was unsure and afraid. Self-doubt pushes you to seek validation from others when it's often unnecessary.

It could be argued that they didn't contribute anything so valuable that I couldn't have managed without it, but having someone cheer me on as I made significant strides was uplifting. Each encouraging conversation boosted my confidence as I ventured into new territory. Reporting back on successful vendor negotiations or adding new elements to design concepts gave me a rush as a key player. It felt like I was accomplishing big things. My immediate circle and family couldn't relate to what was happening in my life, so sharing each twist and turn with a trusted friend felt incredibly satisfying... until they asked for half of my company.

Damn. Ego is expensive.

Now, before you judge me – make sure that you aren't making the same mistakes.

Ask yourself these questions and answer them honestly.

Are you sharing too much too soon?

Are loneliness and isolation leading you to team up with people who don't add real value to your goals?

Are you sure that everyone you talk to about your project understands they're not official consultants for your business?

Are you implementing their ideas without any plans to give them credit?

Have you acted in a way that is not clear regarding what their role is or isn't?

Do you have a contingency plan if they take your ideas and run?

Have you given them access to trade secrets or proprietary details?

Are you at risk of facing revenge if they decide to take that route?

Have you put yourself at risk by trusting someone without fully understanding their intentions?

When you start asking yourself these tough questions, you might realize that I'm not the only one who has shared sensitive insights and business details in an effort to avoid feeling isolated.

They say it's lonely at the top, and I've never been the type of entrepreneur who needed many friends. Having one or two people to bounce ideas off of was always part of my process. Now, I'm learning the hard way that as your business grows and success looms closer, your usual methods might not be enough for the next level.

Success is wonderful, but too much of it can also breed resentment.

People are supportive, up to a point. I've learned this firsthand over the past few weeks.

As I've grown, some have grown uncomfortable with my progress. My excitement, mistaken for arrogance or boasting when all I really hoped for was their support and shared joy.

After all those long nights working on plans while others rested or partied, it's unrealistic to think that those same people who watched you climb will be excited about your success.

This is the point that you are most vulnerable to trusting to soon.

After the isolation starts to break your spirit, finding comfort in a friend can seem like the perfect remedy or so you hope. But even then, you must protect the baby.

Be clear about boundaries and expectations.

After the isolation starts to break your spirit, finding comfort in a friend can seem like the perfect remedy or so you hope. But even then, you must protect the baby.

Trust me. As I watch my phone for updates from suppliers worldwide while typing this book's conclusion, I deeply regret not asking my 'friend' a few tough questions. I wish I had paused, despite my excitement, and said, 'Hey, I want to share something exciting, but what will it cost me?

I might not have liked their response, but at least I wouldn't have someone thinking my brand-new project is also theirs. I also wouldn't be in a position where I'm questioning their integrity, and they're probably questioning mine.

I know I didn't intentionally mislead anyone, but my assumption of their support was neither fair nor correct. Not everyone is on your side just to see you succeed. Some people expect a share of your success. You need to identify those people quickly and clearly, and then stop sharing with them.

I wouldn't have shared a single word with them if I had known how they felt, but here I am. Maybe the signs were there and I missed them. I've been around long enough to know better, but this experience has taught me another important lesson that must be included in this book.

Don't rely on free or familiar help. If you feel lost, take a moment to reassess before giving up, and then hit my new favorite button. **RESET.**

About the Author:

Meet the Author. Koddi Dunn is a highly sought-after business consultant and entrepreneur with over twenty years of executive level experience. She is married to Wade Dunn Jr., and together they have raised 7 children in their blended family.

Koddi Dunn lives in Tulsa, Oklahoma (USA) where she has worked with business, educational, government, non-profit, for profit, and small business agencies from around the world.

Koddi Dunn is the founder and/or managing partner of over a dozen successful and profitable businesses, and she has authored several books on personal and business development.

Follow the Author.

Facebook Fan Page: Facebook.com/KoddiDunn

Instagram: @KoddiDunn

LinkedIn: Linkedin.com/in/KoddiDunn

YouTube Channel: @KoddiDunn

Hire the Author.

For client training, conference speaking, business consulting, and/or booking requests please contact

Pinkrose Marketing LLC, available online at www.PinkroseMarketing.com

Koddi Dunn,

koddi@pinkrosemarketing.com

Pinkrose Marketing LLC

Made in the USA
Middletown, DE
29 July 2024

58091810R00076